WHAT DO YOU DO WITH A VOICE LIKE THAT?

THE STORY OF EXTRAORDINARY CONGRESSWOMAN BARBARA JORDAN

written by
CHRIS BARTON

illustrated by
EKUA HOLMES

Beach Lane Books • New York London Toronto Sydney New Delhi

BEACH LANE BOOKS

An imprint of Simon & Schuster Children's Publishing Division

1230 Avenue of the Americas, New York, New York 10020

For information about special discounts for bulk purchases, please contact Simon & Schuster Special Sales at
1-866-506-1949 or business@simonandschuster.com.

The Simon & Schuster Speakers Bureau can bring authors to your live event. For more information or to book an event,
contact the Simon & Schuster Speakers Bureau at 1-866-248-3049 or visit our website at www.simonspeakers.com.

Book design by Sonia Chaghatzbanian

The text for this book was set in Caxton.

The illustrations for this book were rendered in mixed media.

Manufactured in China

0718 SCP

First Edition

2 4 6 8 10 9 7 5 3 1

Library of Congress Cataloging-in-Publication Data

Names: Barton, Chris, author. | Holmes, Ekua, illustrator.

Title: What do you do with a voice like that? / Chris Barton ; illustrated by Ekua Holmes.

Description: First edition. | New York : Beach Lane Books, [2018] | Includes bibliographical references and index.

Identifiers: LCCN 2017037353 | ISBN 9781481465618 (hardcover : alk. paper) | ISBN 9781481465625 (eBook)

Subjects: LCSH: Jordan, Barbara, 1936–1996—Juvenile literature. | Legislators—United States—Biography—Juvenile literature.
| African American women legislators—Biography—Juvenile literature. | United States. Congress. House—Biography—
Juvenile literature. | African American women legislators—Texas—Biography—Juvenile literature. | Texas—Politics and
government—1951—Juvenile literature. Classification: LCC E840.8.J62 B37 2018 | DDC 328.73/092 [B]—dc23

LC record available at https://lccn.loc.gov/2017037353

For Michael Hurd, Kathi Appelt, and Phil Bildner—
three of my favorite Texans
—C. B.

In memory of my grandparents,
Comado and Queen Hendrix
—E. H.

Growing up in the Fifth Ward of Houston, Texas,
Barbara Jordan stood out.
She may have looked like other kids.
She may have acted like other kids.
But she sure didn't sound like other kids.
Not with that voice of hers.

That *voice*.

That big, bold, booming, crisp, clear, confident voice.
It caused folks to sit right up, stand up straight, and take notice.

What do you *do* with a voice like that?

Well, first you give that voice something to say.
Barbara recited poetry at church.
She memorized speeches for school.
She entered oratory contests and in 1952 won a trip to
Chicago—the first time she'd ever left Texas.
Barbara was proud of herself, and proud of her voice.
It was laying a path for her.

But where would that path lead?

On Sunday evenings, Barbara would talk
things over with Grandpa Patten.

Would she become a preacher like her father,
and like her mother could have been?

Or a teacher, like those who encouraged her
at Phillis Wheatley High?

Or perhaps she'd become a lawyer. Not many
black women had achieved that. But one who
had done so visited Wheatley and gave a
stirring speech.

Barbara was inspired.

Being a lawyer would be a marvelous
use of her voice.
But before that can happen,
what's the *next* thing you do with
a voice like that?

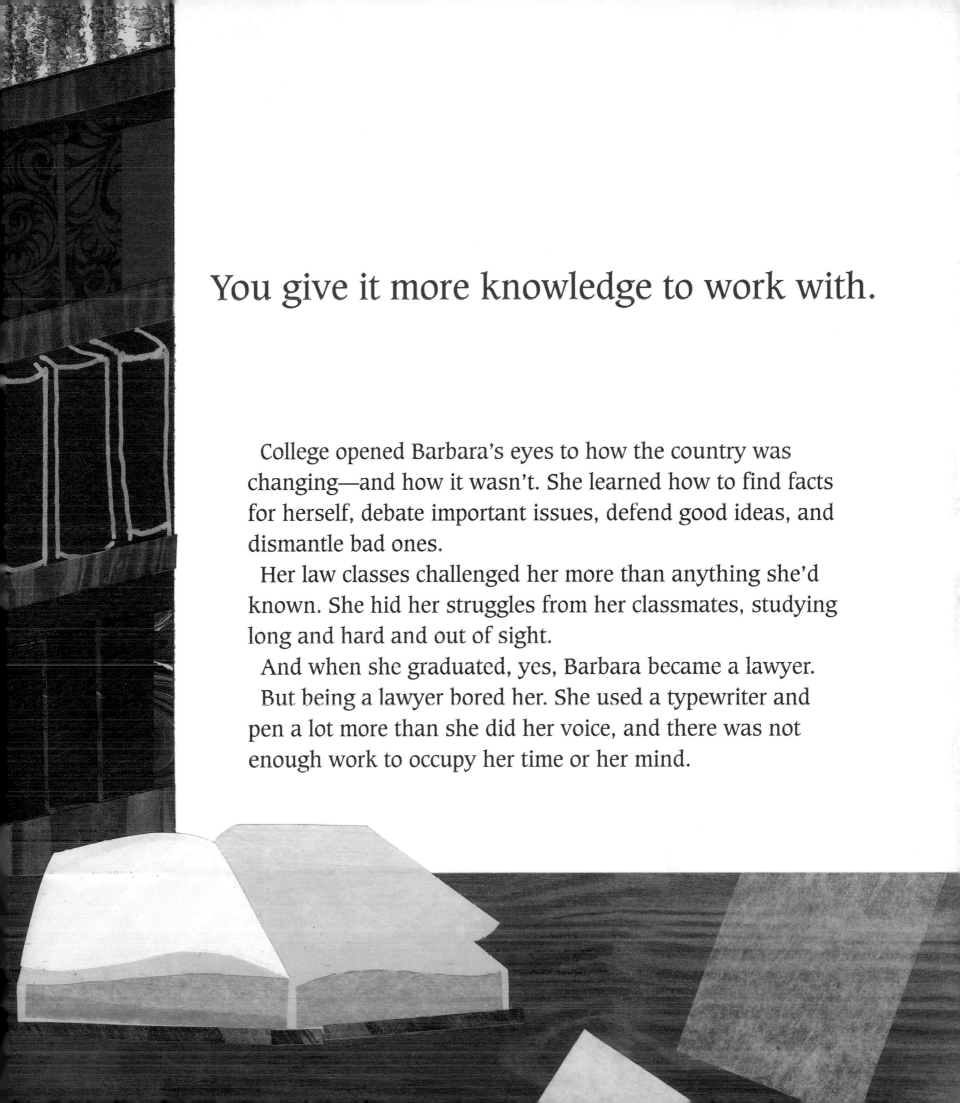

You give it more knowledge to work with.

College opened Barbara's eyes to how the country was changing—and how it wasn't. She learned how to find facts for herself, debate important issues, defend good ideas, and dismantle bad ones.

Her law classes challenged her more than anything she'd known. She hid her struggles from her classmates, studying long and hard and out of sight.

And when she graduated, yes, Barbara became a lawyer.

But being a lawyer bored her. She used a typewriter and pen a lot more than she did her voice, and there was not enough work to occupy her time or her mind.

There was, however, lots of political work that needed doing.

In 1960, America was not as free or as fair a place as it could be. Barbara believed that politics could change that. So she got involved.

One night, a scheduled speaker was absent, and Barbara was asked if she would fill in. She said yes.

The audience loved her. They trusted her. Most important, they were inspired to *do* something—to get out and vote, and to help round up others and get *them* to vote.

Her voice had made a difference.

Barbara, "bitten by the political bug," as she later put it, knew just what to do with a voice like that.

WHY?

WHY?

COALITION BACKS
BARBARA JORDAN

Vote fo
Barb

will get

BECAUSE

LABOR UNIONS
SUPPORT
BARBARA JORDAN

LATIN AMERICANS
SUPPORT
BARBARA JORDAN

NEGRO ORGANIZATION
SUPPORT
BARBARA JORDAN

LIBERAL DEMOCRATS
SUPPORT
BARBARA JORDAN

CITIZENS OF ALL TYPES
SUPPORT
BARBARA JORDAN

A BUCK FOR BARBARA

I'M FOR BARBARA
STATE SENATOR
CITIZENS
ARE? YOU

I'M FOR
BARBA
CONG

She put it to public use.

Barbara wanted more justice and more equality. She knew that these things began with more citizens sharing their own voices with their representatives in government.

To make sure they got heard, Barbara decided to run for political office herself.

So she ran.

And she lost.

And she ran.

And she lost.

"I have no intention of being a three-time loser," she said.

She ran a third time.

This time she won.

As a Texas state senator, Barbara represented the people she'd grown up among. Before, she'd merely trusted in the political system. Now she was part of it.

When it works right, the system makes laws that improve our lives, and it makes sure that people—both the powerful and the powerless—follow those laws.

Changes to our laws sometimes come from raising a ruckus outside the system, but Barbara's way was to make change from within.

Sometimes that change—such as higher pay for farm laborers and more aid for people who got hurt at work—took place in public, through debates on the Senate floor.

Sometimes it didn't.

Barbara got to know the other senators as individuals, and despite their differences, they came to relate to her in the same way. When each listened to what the other had to say, they could hear what was important to them, and it helped them all do a better job.

Other Texans who had never paid any attention to women of color heard the wisdom in her voice, which helped them do better too.

Well, then.

What do you do with a voice like that?

You share it with
the entire country.

In her next election, in 1972,
Barbara moved up to the United
States Congress in Washington, DC.

Soon came a troubled, confusing time for the nation. President Nixon, it seemed, had broken the law, and Congress had to decide what to do about it.

On a TV broadcast seen throughout the country, Barbara used her voice to show them the way. She reminded her audience that the Constitution is the document governing all the laws in the United States and applies to all of its people. Then she explained—in her big, bold, booming, crisp, clear, confident tone—how the president's actions had gone against that document.

"My faith in the Constitution is whole, it is complete, it is total. And I am not going to sit here and be an idle spectator to the diminution, the subversion, the destruction of the Constitution." The Constitution, Barbara said, must be preserved.

The president, Barbara said, must go.

The president went.

That speech
made Barbara
a star.

She shone
like a bright light
in a dark place.

Barbara would have loved
spending more nights under
actual stars, camping and
singing with her friends, but
the public wanted more of her
and more from her.

She delivered, battling to protect the rights of Mexican American voters and others against discrimination.

There were whispers and rumblings of what might be next for Barbara. The US Senate? The Supreme Court? Could she possibly become Vice President Jordan?

Who knew how high she might rise!

So many people had so many hopes for Barbara. In her voice, they knew, there was much to admire.

How she spoke for those who had less power.

How she spoke for those who possessed quieter strengths than her own.

How she spoke for those who did not want to be limited by their weaknesses.

But the public did not know that this last group included Barbara herself, who had been privately struggling with a nerve disease called multiple sclerosis since her earliest days in Congress.

Nor did they know that Barbara had begun hearing another voice.

This other voice was an inner voice.

It instructed her that the right place for Barbara Jordan was not in any of the roles that the public had in mind.

It told Barbara that the right place for her now was as a citizen back home in Texas.

What do you do with a voice like *that*?

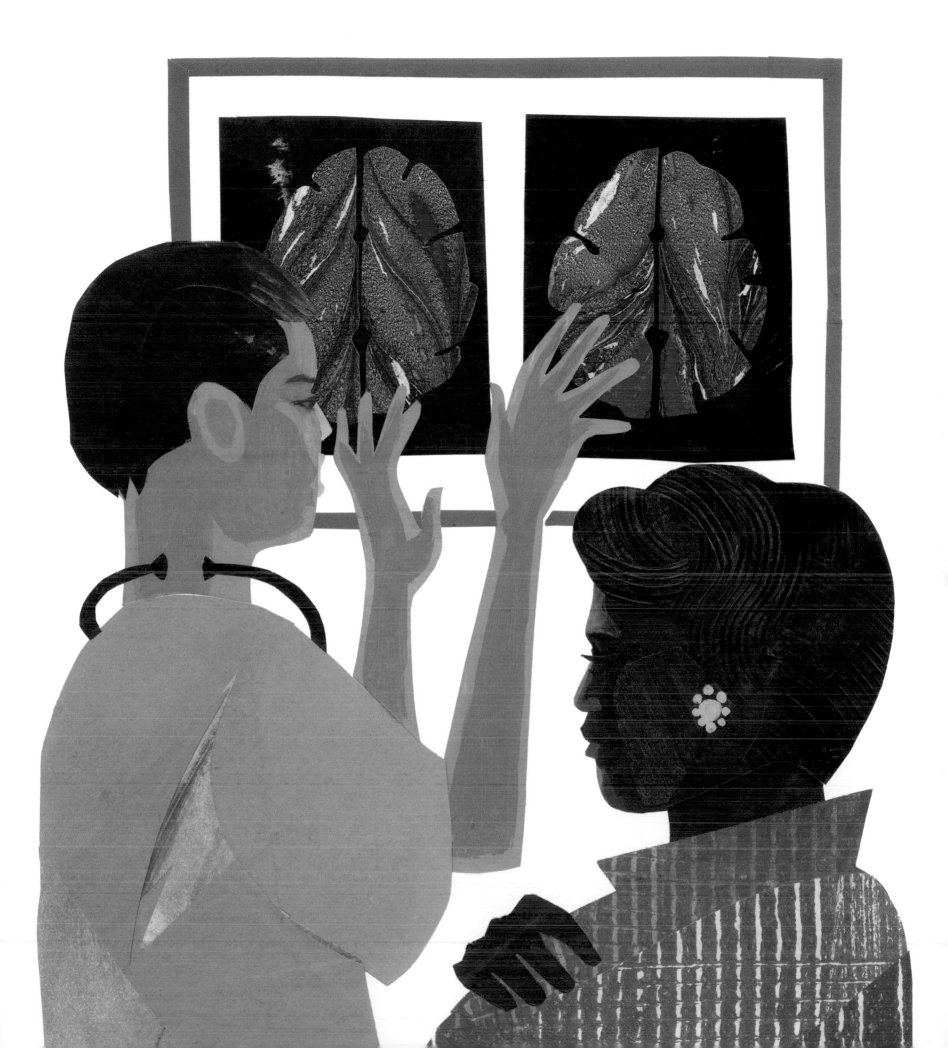

Even as her body failed her, Barbara's mind grew ever wiser,
and she heeded what she heard.

She went home.

There she became a teacher.

College students who intended to put their own voices to public use lined up for the chance to learn from her.

In her classroom, you can bet that they sat right up, stood up straight, and took notice of the values she imparted.

Equality.
Justice.
Trust.

Barbara used her voice to instruct and implore and inspire them not just to get out and *do* something, but to do the *right* thing.

And when the occasion called for it—say, at a basketball game with students such as those she taught, students like Barbara herself once had been—she even used her voice to

raise a ruckus.

Barbara Jordan's former students still move among us, striving to do work that would have made her proud, hearing echoes of her words as they try to make life better for all of us.

For when it has been silenced,

what do we do with a voice like that?

It is logical, simple, and tr

REEDOM

cit ze

the Constitution

In Search of Humanity

nocracy

the great principles of right and wrong

ue.

We remember it,
and we honor it
by making our own
voices heard.

AUTHOR'S NOTE

I began work on this book in 2013, and the years since have been tumultuous ones for the United States. In response to the news of the day, I occasionally ask myself, "What would Barbara Jordan do?"

On one side of Barbara Jordan's tombstone in my home city of Austin, Texas, is the word "Patriot." The other side says "Teacher." I am sorry that her years in each role were cut short. How I wish she had lived to become an octogenarian dispensing the pragmatic insight, moral clarity, and vision of a common good that we and our leaders need today.

But I am so thankful for the many former students of hers, and for the public servants and regular citizens that *they* have influenced and inspired. We are better as a nation for the ripples sent out among us by the example that Barbara Jordan set during her lifetime. May we all honor her memory through teaching and patriotism that are ever more informed, involved, and inclusive.

TIME LINE

1936
Barbara Charline Jordan is born on February 21 in Houston. She is the youngest child of Arlyne (Patten) Jordan and Benjamin Jordan, after sisters Bennie and Rose Mary.

1948–1952
Barbara attends Phillis Wheatley High School. Lawyer Edith Sampson visits Wheatley during Barbara's sophomore year. Her speech inspires Barbara to become an attorney.

The summer after graduation, Barbara wins first place at a national oratorical contest in Chicago.

1952–1956
Barbara attends and graduates from Texas Southern University in Houston. She competes on the award-winning TSU debate team coached by Thomas F. Freeman, who had previously taught Martin Luther King Jr.

1956–1959
Barbara attends law school at Boston University. It is her first experience in a day-to-day environment in which most people she encounters are white.

1960
Barbara returns to Houston and gets involved in the Democratic presidential campaign of John F. Kennedy. Kennedy wins, and Texan Lyndon B. Johnson becomes vice president.

1962
At age twenty-six, Barbara runs in the Democratic primary for a seat in the Texas House of Representatives. She loses.

1964
Barbara loses a second Democratic primary race for state representative.

1974
The House judiciary committee investigates whether President Nixon should be removed from office for violating the Constitution. On July 25, Barbara's remarks on the committee's work ("My faith in the Constitution is whole, it is complete, it is total.") are seen by millions of television viewers. The committee recommends impeaching the president. Nixon resigns on August 9.

In November, Barbara is reelected to a second term.

1975
As part of the renewal of the Voting Rights Act, Barbara successfully leads efforts to add Texas to the states that must get approval of changes to election laws and procedures. Because of her, Spanish-speaking voters in Texas—and speakers of various languages in other states—will no longer be restricted by English-only ballots.

Barbara and Nancy begin the process of buying property together and having a home built.

1976
Barbara gives the keynote speech at the Democratic National Convention. "A spirit of harmony will survive in America," she says, "only if each of us remembers that we share a common destiny; if each of us remembers, when self-interest and bitterness seem to prevail, that we share a common destiny. I have confidence that we can form this kind of national community."

Increasingly reliant on using a cane to walk, Barbara is reelected to Congress for a third term.

1977
Barbara announces that she will not run for reelection the following year. When speaking to reporters about her health, she places her privacy ahead of honesty and mentions only "a bum knee." Barbara says she doesn't know what's next for her, but jokes that she won't be dancing in a Broadway show or playing pro football.

1979
Barbara begins teaching courses in public policy and ethics in government to graduate students at the Lyndon B. Johnson School of Public Affairs at the University of Texas.

1965

President Johnson signs the Voting Rights Act, which eliminates unfair laws in the South that had prevented African Americans from voting. The law requires seven states with histories of discriminating against Black voters to get permission before making changes to voting laws or electoral districts.

1966–67

In November 1966, Barbara wins election to the Texas Senate. She becomes the first African American woman ever in the Texas legislature. The thirty other state senators are all white men.

During the 1967 legislative session, Barbara is invited to the White House to discuss civil rights with President Johnson. They become friends.

1968–69

In November 1968, Barbara is reelected to a four-year term. President Johnson is succeeded by Republican Richard Nixon.

In the 1969 legislative session Barbara sponsors successful bills increasing compensation for injured workers and establishing a minimum wage for agricultural workers.

On a camping trip with mutual friends, Barbara meets psychologist Nancy Earl, who becomes her lifelong companion.

1972

On June 17, five men working on behalf of President Nixon's reelection campaign break into the Democratic National Committee's office at the Watergate building in Washington, DC.

In November, Barbara wins a seat in the US House of Representatives. She becomes one of the first two African Americans elected to Congress from the South in seventy years.

1973

On the advice of former President Johnson, Barbara seeks and receives an appointment to the House Judiciary Committee. Throughout the year, investigations into the Watergate break-in reveal President Nixon's efforts to cover up his administration's wrongdoing.

Barbara experiences numbness and tingling in her feet and hands, and weakness in her legs. After she is hospitalized in December, doctors identify multiple sclerosis as the likely cause.

EARLY 1980S

While keeping details about her health private, Barbara switches to a walker and then a wheelchair to help her get around.

1988

Barbara nearly drowns after losing consciousness in her swimming pool. News reports about the accident reveal her multiple sclerosis to the public.

1992

Barbara gives a speech at what will be her final Democratic National Convention. She calls for a social and political environment "which is characterized by a devotion to the public interest, public service, tolerance, and love. Love. Love. Love."

1993–94

Barbara is appointed chair of the bipartisan Commission on Immigration Reform by President Bill Clinton. The commission recommends reducing both legal and illegal immigration by addressing conditions in would-be migrants' home countries, modernizing systems and regulations, and rigorously enforcing the law.

President Clinton awards Barbara the Presidential Medal of Freedom, the highest award for American civilians.

1996

Barbara plans to begin her eighteenth year of teaching. But on January 17, suffering from multiple sclerosis, leukemia, and pneumonia, she dies in Austin at age 59.

"Through the sheer force of the truth she spoke, the poetry of her words, and the power of her voice, Barbara always stirred our national conscience," President Clinton says at her funeral. "When Barbara Jordan talked, we listened."

RECOMMENDED VIEWING AND READING

A great first step for learning more about Barbara Jordan is to watch or listen to online videos of her 1974 speech during the House Judiciary Committee presidential impeachment hearings and her 1976 keynote address to the Democratic National Convention.

The best biography of Barbara Jordan written for an adult audience is *Barbara Jordan: American Hero* by Mary Beth Rogers.

Other suggested books for understanding Barbara Jordan's life and times include:

Blaise, Misha Maynerick. *This Is Texas, Y'All!: The Lone Star State from A to Z.* Guilford, Connecticut: Lone Star Books, 2017.

Corey, Shana, and R. Gregory Christie. *A Time to Act: John F. Kennedy's Big Speech.* New York: NorthSouth Books, 2017.

Oelschlager, Vanita, and Joe Rossi. *The Electrifying Story of Multiple Sclerosis.* New York: VanitaBooks, 2015.

Pohlen, Jerome. *Gay & Lesbian History for Kids: The Century-Long Struggle for LGBT Rights.* Chicago: Chicago Review Press, 2015.

Sheinkin, Steve. *Most Dangerous: Daniel Ellsberg and the Secret History of the Vietnam War.* New York: Roaring Brook Press, 2015.

Winegarten, Ruthe, and Sharon Kahn. *Brave Black Women: From Slavery to the Space Shuttle.* Austin: The University of Texas Press, 1997.

Winter, Jonah, and Shane W. Evans. *Lillian's Right to Vote: A Celebration of the Voting Rights Act of 1965.* New York: Schwartz & Wade Books, 2015.

A complete bibliography for this book is available at chrisbarton.info/books/barbarajordan.